KILLER BUGS

Other **STRANGER THAN FICTION** *Books by*
Melvin Berger
Coming Soon from Avon Camelot

DINOSAURS
MONSTERS
SEA MONSTERS

MELVIN BERGER is the author of over 100 books
for young readers. He was born in New York City
and has received degrees from the University of
Rochester, Columbia University, and London University. He was elected to the New York Academy
of Sciences in 1983.

His books have won many awards and honors and
have been translated into 22 languages. Mr. Berger lives in Great Neck, New York, with his wife
Gilda, who is also an author of books for young
people. The Bergers are the parents of two grown
daughters.

STRANGER THAN FICTION

KILLER BUGS

MELVIN BERGER

Pictures by Kelly Oechsli

AN AVON CAMELOT BOOK

KILLER BUGS is an original publication of Avon Books. This work has never before appeared in book form.

AVON BOOKS
A division of
The Hearst Corporation
105 Madison Avenue
New York, New York 10016

First Avon Camelot Printing: October 1990

CAMELOT TRADEMARK REG. U.S. PAT. OFF. AND IN OTHER COUNTRIES, MARCA REGISTRADA, HECHO EN U.S.A.

Printed in the U.S.A.

OPM 10 9 8 7 6 5 4 3 2 1

CONTENTS

STRANGER THAN FICTION

KILLER BUGS

INTRODUCTION

- More people are killed by bugs than by all other animals combined—including snakes and sharks!
- Every year millions suffer bug bites or stings—and many thousands die as a result!
- Most bugs are tiny—not even one inch long and weighing less than an ounce. Yet they can kill humans many times their size and weight!

The most damaging of the harmful bugs are called "killer bugs." Their stories are amazing. Many are truly *stranger than fiction*!

If you're like most people, you find bugs annoying. You don't enjoy the sight or sound of bugs buzzing around a room or a picnic table. You don't want to eat food after a bug has landed on it. And you hate the pain or itch that comes after a bug bite.

But do you know that bugs can also be very dangerous? And do you know how and why killer bugs act the way they do?

Basically, there are two kinds of harmful bugs. Those that bite with their mouths, and those that sting with rear-end stingers.

1

Bugs that bite have special mouth parts. Some, like army ants, feed on solid food. They have two jaws sticking out front. These jaws are like claws. They grab bits of food and push them into the mouth.

Others, like bees, spiders, and flies, dine only on liquids. Part of their mouth is a tube, like a short, thin drinking straw. The tube usually has a sharp point that can pierce through skin.

Some biting bugs, like fleas and mosquitoes, may carry disease-causing germs. When they attack, the germs get into the victim's body. The germs multiply and make the person very sick, and sometimes even cause death.

Dangerous bugs that sting are equipped with stingers—hollow tubes with sharp points. The bug drills the point down into the flesh of the victim. Wasps paralyze their prey with their stings. Bees leave their stingers in the skin of the victim to do even more harm.

The bites or stings of killer bugs often force poison, or venom, into the wound. The venom is a hurtful chemical. It causes the pain and other bad reactions that may follow a bug attack.

Scientists know of more than one million different kinds of bugs in the world. They suspect that the number may be even higher. And there are billions and billions of each kind. In fact, there are more bugs on earth than all other animals put together!

But of all these bugs, only a small number actually kills people. The fly walking up a wall, the ant crawling along the ground, the spider spinning its web, the mosquito buzzing around a room—these are not killers. Only a very few are dangerous and need to be avoided.

Before we meet the killer bugs, let's take a moment to find out more about bugs in general.

WHAT ARE BUGS?

Bugs is a common name for many different kinds of small, creepy, crawly, and flying animals. Some bugs—such as ants, bees, wasps, and hornets—are insects. Other bugs—such as spiders and scorpions—are arachnids.

All insects are the same in a few ways. They all have six legs. And they all have bodies that are divided into three parts.

The front part of the insect body is the head. It contains the brain, the eyes, and the mouth parts. Attached to the head are the feelers or antennae.

Behind the head is the middle part or thorax. The insect's legs are attached to the thorax. If the insect has wings, they are attached here, too.

The back part of the insect is the abdomen. The organs for digestion and reproduction are found here. And in many insects the stinger is at the back end of the abdomen.

Insects are the same in still another way. They pass through similar life stages. Insects are born from eggs. When the eggs hatch, which may be only a few hours after being laid, the larvae appear. The larvae look like little worms or caterpillars.

In the next stage, the larvae spin cocoons and

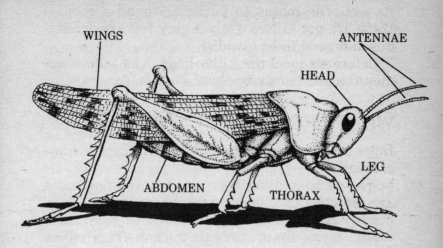

WINGS

ANTENNAE

HEAD

LEG

ABDOMEN

THORAX

AN INSECT

disappear inside. They are now pupae. Finally, the pupae force their way out of the cocoons. They emerge as full grown insects.

As we said, spiders and scorpions are arachnids. They look and act like insects, but in some ways they are different.

Spiders and scorpions:

- have eight legs instead of six.
- don't have antennae or wings.
- have two body parts instead of three (the head and thorax are in one part; the abdomen is separate).

FRIENDS OR FOES?

Bugs are important to us because they eat so much. They are always hunting for food. Along the way, they sometimes serve humans as well.

Bees, for example, sip nectar, the tiny drops of liquid found in flower blossoms. As they do, they produce honey and carry pollen from flower to flower. Without pollen most flowers cannot produce seeds.

Wasps and spiders prey on insects. In the process they help rid us of many insect pests.

When ants go into their nests to feed their young, they tunnel through the soil. This mixes the earth and makes it better for farming.

Only fleas, flies, mosquitoes, and a few other insects feed on human blood. Almost none eat human flesh.

Why, then, do bugs bite and sting humans?

Why are there killer bugs?

Some bugs seem to bite and sting for no reason. They are very aggressive and are always ready to swoop down on their victims.

But most bugs strike at humans only when they sense danger. They attack if someone comes near, or frightens, disturbs, or touches them. If people don't bother these bugs, the bugs won't bother them. Bugs usually flee rather than go after a human being.

The chances of getting sick or of dying from a bug bite or sting are very small. In fact, the odds are better that you'll win the lottery or be struck by lightning than meet up with a killer bug. Still, it's fun to know about killer bugs—what they are, how they live, and the harm they do. Perhaps you'll agree that they are among the strangest and most fascinating beings on earth.

KILLER BEES

ATTACK OF THE KILLER BEES

On September 6, 1972, the six children of José and Dora de Lima were playing in the backyard of their home in Austim, a suburb of Sâo Paulo, Brazil. Their parents were out shopping. One youngster became curious about a beehive that his father had placed on a tree a few days before. He poked the hive with a small stick.

Instantly, hundreds of noisy bees swarmed out of the hive. Soaring swiftly in a zigzag flight pattern, the bees buzzed toward the de Lima children. Within seconds, the agitated insects settled on the children's faces, arms, and legs. Some even flew into the little ones' mouths, ears, and noses. Everywhere the horrible insects landed, they dug in their sharp stingers.

With shrieks and wild slaps the children tried to ward off the vicious attackers. But their attempts were in vain. The swats and swipes just drove the stingers down deeper.

A neighbor, Mrs. Anita Damasceno, heard the children's shrill cries. She rushed to their aid and carried, dragged, and pushed them into her house.

Working as fast as she could, Mrs. Damasceno removed all the bees and pulled out their stingers.

But Mrs. Damasceno could do little for the painful bites on the children's swollen arms, legs, and faces. She couldn't relieve the hurting eyes, which were just narrow slits in the children's puffed-up faces. And there was no way to soothe their swollen lips—as big and red as ripe plums.

The ambulance Mrs. Damasceno called to the scene rushed the children to the hospital. Sydney, aged seven, who had received about 60 stings, was in the worst shape. Despite the doctors' best efforts, he died soon afterwards. The others recovered. After a few days in the hospital they were able to return home.

The de Lima parents blamed themselves for the terrible tragedy. The distraught father made a torch from a rolled-up newspaper and burned down the beehive.

Mr. de Lima later explained that he and his wife had found the hive while walking in the woods. The hive had fallen out of a tree and was still full of bees. The couple decided to take the hive home and collect the honey.

Experts told de Lima that the bees were no ordinary honeybees. They were, in fact, killer bees!

WHAT ARE KILLER BEES?

Killer bees (scientific name—*Apis mellifera scutellata*) are very close relatives of the ordinary honeybee. In some ways they are the same. But in other ways they are quite different.

Most people know the ordinary honeybee. It is

Honeybee sipping nectar from an apple blossom
Negative No. 324029; courtesy Department Library Services, American
Museum of Natural History

the best-known of all kinds of bees. That is because honeybees are found all over the world—except in the very cold areas around the North and South Poles.

The honeybee's body ranges from black to dark brown with yellow stripes. Its head is blunt and studded with thousands of tiny eyes—even though the bee can't see very well.

Two antennae are also on the head. They give the bee its sense of smell and sense of touch. The bee uses its long, hollow tongue to sip nectar from flowers. When not in use, the tongue curls back under the head. Attached to the thorax are four wings for flying. And a barbed stinger is hidden in the rear end of the abdomen.

Honeybees live in large colonies. Their nests, or hives, contain up to 70,000 bees. The bees in one hive could fill all the seats in Yankee Stadium or Dodger Stadium—with nearly 20,000 bees left over!

Every day honeybees fly from flower to flower collecting pollen and nectar. Chemicals in their stomach change the nectar into honey. When they fly back to the hive they put the drops of honey into special cells inside the nest. The honey is food for the young bees.

Killer bees have the same yellow stripes on their bodies as regular honeybees. Killer bees, though, are a little smaller and weigh a bit less.

Like honeybees, they live in hives. And they too collect nectar from flowers to make honey.

The wings of killer bees beat faster. Their buzz is at a higher pitch. And they fly at a higher speed than the others. When flying, they follow zigzag patterns instead of flying in straight lines like ordinary honeybees.

Also, killer bees don't stay very long in one nest. They are always on the move. If something disturbs their nest, they swarm out in gigantic numbers and set up another nest in a tree, a cave, or even a hole in the ground.

In order to survive in Africa, where they have many natural enemies, killer bees have become much fiercer and more savage than ordinary honeybees. They are very nervous, quick to attack and sting at any time.

Killer bees will sting their victims for almost any reason. If someone touches or shakes a killer bee hive—the bees swarm out and attack. If someone just walks with a heavy step or shouts near their hive—the bees attack. Even if someone just gets too close to killer bees as they fly from flower to flower—they attack.

And when they attack, they are out to kill.

In a typical killer bee attack, up to 1,000 buzzing bees charge at the offender. Wave after wave of furious insects push and shove to reach their target. Soon, a live, wiggling blanket of bees covers the victim's body.

Each attacking bee has a powerful stinger tucked away at the rear of its abdomen. The stinger is a sharp, pointed, hollow tube. It is about one-tenth of an inch long. As the bee lands, it lowers the back of its body onto the victim and plunges in the stinger. The tip of the spear-like stinger easily cuts right through layers of clothing and skin.

Through their stingers the bees pump venom

into their victims. Once they are dug into the skin, the stingers are very hard to pull out. Each stinger has barbs, like a fishhook. The barbs grab on to the flesh and stay in place. Even when the bee flies off, the stinger remains stuck in the wound.

The barbs hurt the victim. By holding the stinger fast, they let the bee pump more and more venom into the wound. But the barbs are also bad for the bee. Without its stinger, the bee can live for only an hour or so before it dies.

Even though each killer bee can sting only once, many bees often attack at the same time, leaving the victim with a large number of stings.

The venom of the killer bee is about four times as powerful and harmful as the poison of a cobra snake! It is so strong that it raises angry red welts on the skin at once. The redness and swelling are actually caused by the venom starting to dissolve the victim's flesh.

At the very least, killer bee stings hurt and make their victims feel itchy and very tense. But some people are allergic to all bee venom. They have a bad reaction to even one sting. When they are stung they find it hard to breathe and swallow. They also feel nauseous and are likely to throw up. Dizziness and strong pains in the abdomen may also follow.

Many become unable to speak. They feel weak and confused. In the most severe cases, the victims can die within 10 or 15 minutes unless they take antivenom medicine that they carry with them or get to a doctor immediately.

Killer bee stings can be life threatening, even to people who are not allergic to bee stings. Any person who gets 50 or more killer bee stings may fall into a state of shock. His blood pressure falls. His face turns pale or bluish. And the person collapses and becomes unconscious. At this point, only quick medical care can save his life.

It is almost impossible to escape the attack of killer bees. Some people try to run away as fast as they can. But the bees are even speedier. They can fly at 12 miles an hour—which is faster than most humans can run. And they are stubborn. They don't let anyone get away. Killer bees have been known to give chase for over a mile! That is much, much farther than any other insect will stalk its prey.

One scientist wanted to see how aggressive

killer bees really are. He planned to dangle a piece of leather in front of a hive for 30 seconds. Later, he would count the number of stings in the leather.

The scientist put on especially heavy protective clothes. He then shook a hive of killer bees while holding the leather. As expected, the bees instantly swarmed out in a stinging frenzy.

Even in his protective suit the scientist was terrified by the fury of the attack. After only five seconds, he gave up the experiment and ran off. He fled for over a mile with the huge pack of bees in close pursuit.

In time the killer bees gave up the chase. The scientist returned to examine the piece of leather. To his amazement, he found that the bees had stung the leather 92 times in just the first five seconds!

WHERE DO KILLER BEES COME FROM?

Killer bees were once found only in Africa. Today they also live in Brazil and other countries of South America. And they are traveling north. The story of their spread from Africa to South America and points north is quite amazing.

Dr. Warwick Kerr, a scientist at the University of Sâo Paulo in Brazil, was an expert on honeybees. In 1956 he was trying to find a way to get more honey from the honeybees that lived in Brazil.

Dr. Kerr had an idea. He knew that the honeybees in Africa made much more honey than the ones in Brazil. African bees start gathering nectar from flowers around an hour earlier in the morn-

Swarm of honeybees
Courtesy Grant Heilman Photography, Inc.

ing than Brazilian honeybees. And they keep flitting from flower to flower up to an hour later in the evening. Also, they go out on rainy days when most honeybees stay in their nests.

But Dr. Kerr also knew something else. African bees are much more dangerous than Brazilian bees. They sting more often. They sting without reason. And their stings are much more deadly. That's why Africans call them killer bees.

Still, Dr. Kerr wondered what would happen if he crossed the easygoing—but lazy—Brazilian bees with the mean—but hardworking—African bees. Would he get bees that produced more honey and were not too mean?

Off to Africa he went. He collected 133 of the gentlest bees he could find. His scheme was to bring them back to Brazil where they would lay their eggs. When the eggs hatched he would allow the African bees to mate with native bees. Then he would see if the new bees made lots of honey— and were not too dangerous.

Dr. Kerr stayed on in Africa while he shipped the bees back to Brazil. He sent them by way of Lisbon, Portugal. When the box with the bees was passing through customs in Portugal, an official heard the loud buzzing. He became frightened and sprayed the box with an insecticide. The chemical killed all the African bees.

Dr. Kerr was still in Africa when he heard what had happened. Not wanting to return home empty-handed, he caught another 70 African bees. But this time he was in a hurry. He didn't take the time to pick only gentle ones. Many of the bees he captured were extremely vicious.

Forty-seven of these African bees survived the trip back to Brazil. Dr. Kerr placed them in his hives. He was just about ready to start his experiment, when something terrible happened. A friend, who was also a beekeeper, accidentally left open the door to the hives. Twenty-six of the African bees escaped.

Very quickly, the African honeybees began mating with the native honeybees. The offspring, or crossbreeds, were a new kind of honeybee.

The beekeepers of Brazil soon noticed a change. And they were very happy. The crossbreeds, they found, were producing about twice as much honey as the Brazilian bees.

The public, though, was troubled. More and more people were being stung by the crossbreeds. And some people were dying from the stings.

As time went on, the wild African bees were spreading like a forest fire across the country. In little more than ten years, the African bees had taken over. There were more of them in Brazil than any other kind of wild bee.

Why did the African bees spread so quickly in Brazil?

First, they had no natural enemies. Animals that killed and ate them in Africa were left behind. Free from danger, they were able to multiply without limit.

And second, they reproduced much faster than the native bees. Brazilian honeybee queens lay between 1,500 and 3,000 eggs daily. African queens lay up to 5,000 eggs a day.

Bit by bit, the situation grew worse. The crossbreeds in Brazil were proving to be dangerous and deadly. There was no way to control their breeding. Their bad qualities had taken over. The cross-breeds had become killer bees.

WHAT DOES THE FUTURE HOLD?

At present, killer bee stings lead to between 50 and 500 deaths every year. The experts are not sure of the exact number. Many deaths from bee stings are probably never reported. And countless bee sting deaths are blamed on heart attacks or heatstroke by mistake. The symptoms are very much the same.

But the experts agree that the number of killer bees—and the number of attacks—is on the rise. From 1957 until the 1970s, killer bees spread throughout Brazil. Then, slowly, they began moving north. By the early 1980s, they were becoming pests in Venezuela and Colombia, too. Since then they have made their way up through Central America and into Mexico.

Experts estimate that the bees are now heading toward the United States at a rate of about 300 miles a year. By the mid–1990s killer bees will almost surely be in Texas.

In 1985 there was a big scare in California. A colony of killer bees was found in the Lost Hills oilfield about 150 miles north of Los Angeles. Scientists think they came on a ship carrying lumber from South America to the west coast of the United States.

The federal government sprang into action. Very quickly they destroyed the 12 swarms of killer bees that were nesting there.

Scientists are now trying to head off the invasion of killer bees. They are looking for natural enemies of killer bees. They are also searching for sprays or other ways to get rid of them, without harming other living animals and plants.

A major breakthrough came in October 1989. A scientist invented a device that can tell whether a bee is a plain honeybee or a killer bee. You know that killer bees beat their wings faster than honeybees and make a higher buzz. This new invention listens for the buzz. A higher buzz signals a killer bee. Identifying killer bees is the first step in controlling them.

Bee experts are on the lookout for killer bees. They fear that if these bees invade America, the number of deaths will go way up. The present plan is to try to stop the killer bees before they reach our borders. If not, scientists hope to check them before they spread.

It's war! And the experts are doing everything in their power to keep out the killer bees!

2

FIRE ANTS

ATTACK OF THE FIRE ANTS

Sixth grader Sally Thomas left her home in Dallas, Texas, early on April 6, 1988. She arrived at school a short while later. Little did she know what a horrible tragedy awaited her.

During her lunchtime recess, Sally was playing soccer with some friends in the school yard. A wild kick sent the ball flying. The ball went bouncing off the field. It landed in a distant part of the school yard. The spot was far from where the children usually played.

No one went to this far-off corner because a number of fire ant mounds dotted the area. These piles of dirt made it hard to walk or run there. Also, the teachers had warned the students to stay away because fire ants are dangerous.

As Sally ran to get the ball she had kicked, she tripped on one of the mounds. Since she was running at full speed, the girl slammed down hard on the anthill. She lay there for a minute gasping for breath. Instantly hundreds of ants poured out of the mound and began to creep all over her bare arms and legs.

Sally's shrieks let everyone know that the fire ants were stinging. The stings, like red-hot needles being jabbed into her skin, made Sally writhe and thrash about on the ground.

Within a minute her teacher, Mr. Frank Kenso, and other students were at Sally's side. Quickly, they helped her up and began to pick off the attacking ants.

In a short while, the badly shaken girl was free of the savage insects. Mr. Kenso led her away from the mound and toward the school building.

Suddenly Sally stopped and tottered on her feet. "I feel sick," she said weakly to Mr. Kenso. "I think I may throw up." Mr. Kenso saw that she had turned a ghostly white.

"It's only a little farther," Mr. Kenso urged. "We'll get you to the nurse's office. She'll take care of you. You'll be able to rest there."

Sally gasped, "But—but I can't breathe!" And she fell to the ground in a dead faint. Her arms and legs were shaking and twitching out of control.

"Call an ambulance!" Mr. Kenso shouted as he covered Sally's trembling body with his suit jacket.

The ambulance arrived 12 minutes after receiving the emergency call. But by the time the doctor examined Sally, it was too late. She was dead.

The medical reports show that Sally was highly allergic to the venom in ant stings. She had been stung between 40 and 50 times in the minute she lay on the mound. And her severe reaction to all that ant venom had killed her.

WHAT ARE FIRE ANTS?

Fire ants (*Solenopsis invicta*) look like ordinary house ants, except that the fire ants are a dull red color. They are about the same size, usually no more than a quarter-inch long. That's about as long as the fingernail on your little finger.

It's their sting that sets fire ants apart from house ants. At best, the fire ant sting hurts. At the very worst, it can kill.

Fire ants usually live in colonies or nests of over 100,000 ants. That's as many individuals as in a small city. Places like Miami Beach, New Haven, Peoria, Bakersfield, and Duluth each have a population of around 100,000.

The nests of the fire ants are mounds of soil on the ground. The mounds can be as big as three feet across and up to three feet tall.

When scientists cut open one of these mounds they find a maze of tunnels and small rooms or chambers. Somewhere inside one of the tunnels or chambers they find the queen ant.

The queen ant is a very special female ant. She is much larger than all the others. In fact, she is so big and heavy that she can't move around or do anything by herself. The queen's only job is to lay eggs.

A flock of small ants surround the queen. They feed her and carry her from place to place. These helper ants, all female, are called worker ants.

Other female worker ants do the rest of the work in the colony. They build and care for the mound. They find food and feed the young. And they guard the colony against all enemies. When someone disturbs the nest, the workers launch the attack.

Perhaps 100 of the female ants in the nest have wings. In time, these ants will become queens. When they do, they fly off and start their own colonies. Once they are queen ants, their wings break off. They remain wingless for the rest of their lives.

A few thousand male ants, who keep their wings, also live in the same colony. But they are not around very long. Male ants do not do any work in the nest. Their main job is to mate with the queen. Soon after mating, they wander away from the colony and die.

Although they have eyes, ants are nearly blind. They can see only the difference between light and dark. Their two antennae help them to smell, feel, and taste the things around them. Without their antennae, the ants are helpless.

How then do ants keep in touch with each other? They use their fine sense of smell.

Suppose a person comes near a mound. Worker ants guarding the entrance smell someone approaching. They immediately release an alarm odor. The smell warns the others of danger.

In a flash, dozens—or hundreds—of ants surge out of the nest. Each heads straight for the intruder. And each looks for a spot to sting.

Fire ants also use smell in another way. It helps them in their never-ending hunt for food.

A worker ant finds a big dead caterpillar. She nips off a bit of its flesh with her jaws. Even though it weighs more than she does, the worker ant drags the morsel of food back to the nest.

As she makes her way to the nest, she leaves a smell trail. Now other worker ants can follow the trail back to the caterpillar. And each one will take another bite and bring it to the nest.

Fire ants, like most other ants, are very strong. These tiny creatures weigh about 1/100th of an ounce. That's as much as a pinch of salt. But they can carry loads that are 50 times heavier than themselves!

HOW DO FIRE ANTS KILL?

The attack of the fire ant is a two-step operation. First, the fire ant climbs onto its victim. It snaps open its long, mean-looking jaws. WHAP! Like sharp scissors closing, the jaws slam shut deep in the skin of the victim.

Then, with its jaws locked securely in place, the ant is ready to sting. It lowers its rear end and stabs the victim with its stinger. Through the hollow center of the stinger it injects a dose of poison.

Chemicals in the poison enter the victim's body. Some of them cause great pain. They make the skin feel as though someone is holding a burning match against it.

After stinging, the fire ant still holds on to the victim with its jaws. But now it circles a little with its rear end. It digs in its stinger again. And it shoots in another dose of poison. On and on it goes—wiggle-sting, wiggle-sting, wiggle-sting.

Soon the deed is done. A dot in the middle shows where the ant clamped its jaws in the skin. Surrounding the bite is a small circle of bright red sting marks.

In a couple of hours the burning pain stops. Then large blisters form and the skin becomes sore and tender.

In ten hours or so, the blisters fill with cloudy pus. At this stage, even a light pat on the skin makes the victim yelp in agony.

Most of the pus-filled blisters pop and heal in about a week. A few form white scars that may stay forever.

Eighty-five out of every 100 people stung by fire ants suffer only the pain and maybe some permanent scars. The other 15 are far less lucky. These are the ones who are allergic to fire ant venom. They can become very sick. Some, like Sally Thomas, may die within minutes of the stings.

For those with an allergy to ant venom, the fire ant sting can trigger a whole range of symptoms. Among the most common are wheezing, dizziness, trouble breathing, and a rash or hives. Stomach pains, nausea and vomiting, and difficulty in thinking clearly and concentrating are not unusual. In the most severe cases, the blood pressure drops very low and the person passes into shock, and may die.

Fire ants sting close to five million people in the United States every year. All suffer the fierce burning pain of the sting and the discomfort of the blisters. About 85,000 end up in a doctor's office or hospital emergency room. Perhaps a dozen or so actually die from the stings.

WHAT DOES THE FUTURE HOLD?

Until 1940 there were no red fire ants in America. Then the first of these pests arrived, probably on a ship carrying lumber from Brazil to Mobile, Alabama. Today fire ants cover about 400 million acres of land in the United States. They live in nine states—from Florida in the east to Texas in the west; from Alabama in the south to North Carolina in the north.

Once they got here, the red fire ants multiplied very quickly. They have no natural enemies. And no chemical spray has been found that can control these killer insects without poisoning the land.

Only one thing seems to stop red fire ants. It is cold weather. Fire ants can't live where the temperature drops below 10° Fahrenheit. Thus people north of the Mason-Dixon Line have little to worry about.

The situation is worse for folks living in the western United States. Fire ants now seem to be moving west in the direction of California at the rate of about 15 miles a year. Many in their path are afraid of these deadly insects. They fear its sting. But they have other concerns as well.

Fire ants kill small animals, such as rabbits and chickens. These insects inject so much venom that they have even killed young cows, goats, and pigs! Such farm animals and pets are sometimes tied to posts or held in pens. They can't escape a mass attack by fire ants. Some animals, like calves, tend to freeze in place when being attacked. This makes them easy victims for the vicious fire ants.

Fire ants also eat most anything. Their basic diet is usually grasshoppers, caterpillars, and worms. But they are happy to feed on plants, including crops growing on farms.

The nests the fire ants build tend to ruin the land for farming. Unlike many other kinds of ants, fire ant nests form hard, tall mounds of dirt. Nothing grows from the mound. And its hardness make plowing and working the land very difficult. For these reasons farmers, more than others, keep a sharp eye out for these dread pests.

A survey in Florida showed the extent of the fire ant problem. Areas infested with fire ants may have as many as 500 mounds and between 8 and 23 million fire ants per acre!

The fire ants' close cousins, the harvester ants, are almost as troublesome.

WHAT ARE HARVESTER ANTS?

Harvester ants look like fire ants. They also behave in much the same way. And when they attack, their sting is just as hurtful and their venom is just as deadly.

The nests of harvester ants are unlike those of fire ants. Harvester ant mounds are flat or only bulge slightly above the ground. Surrounding the nest is a patch of dry soil that covers a circle anywhere from two to ten feet in diameter. No grass or plants of any kind can grow in the soil around the harvester ant nest.

Harvester ants are mostly found in the southwestern corner of the United States. Some mounds, though, can be seen as far east as Kansas.

The poison of the harvester ant is exceedingly powerful and deadly. At one time, the Apache Indians of the American southwest used it to punish prisoners in a most horrible way. They would tie prisoners sentenced to death on the ground over a harvester ant nest. And they would leave the prisoners there until the ants killed them.

Scientists would like to find some way to guard humans and their pets against the poisonous stings of harvester ants. Late in 1989, someone found a substance in horned lizards that protects the lizards from the sting. Now experts are studying the substance. They hope to make a safe and effective drug that will protect humans against the stings of harvester ants, as well as fire ants.

3

ARMY ANTS

ATTACK OF THE ARMY ANTS

Dr. David Livingstone, the well-known African explorer, barely survived a most grisly attack by droves of army ants. The assault occurred on February 18, 1873, at Mr. Livingstone's remote jungle camp near Lake Tanganyika, Africa.

Dr. Livingstone became famous after he was found deep in the African jungle by the reporter Henry Stanley. The newsman had been searching for the explorer over a period of eight months. When they finally met, they were the only people for miles and miles around. Yet Stanley found it necessary to greet him with the words that are so often quoted: "Dr. Livingstone, I presume?"

The night the army ants invaded Dr. Livingstone's camp, he was asleep in his tent. About midnight he was awakened by a soft hissing sound. He lit a candle. To his horror, he saw several long, thick columns of dreaded army ants threading their way into his tent. One line of ants had climbed up a leg of his bed. And they were heading across the sheet in his direction!

Dr. Livingstone lay still and unmoving. He had

been told that if he didn't frighten or disturb them, the ants would not bite. But that proved to be wrong. As he lay there, motionless, the ants struck.

"They first came on my foot quietly," wrote Dr. Livingstone. "Then some began to bite between the toes. The larger ones swarmed over the foot and began to bite fiercely and make the blood start out."

Dr. Livingstone jumped out of bed and stumbled outside. Hordes of ants filled the space around his tent. "My whole person was instantly covered," he went on. Hundreds of ants were crawling all over him, sinking their razor-sharp jaws into his exposed skin.

Some army ants had also invaded the tents of Dr. Livingstone's staff. A few workers became frightened and fled into the jungle. Others stayed to help. They lit grass fires to drive away the advancing ants.

By the light of the blazing grass, Dr. Livingstone's helpers rushed to his side. They started pulling off the vicious ants. "My men picked some off my limbs and tried to save me," he reported. "After battling for an hour or two they took me to a hut not yet invaded."

Exhausted from the struggle to free himself from the warring ants, Dr. Livingstone lay limply on the bed. After a few moments he again heard the quiet rustling sound of army ants on the march.

Moving stiffly from the pain, Dr. Livingstone made his way outside. A steady tropical rain was falling. He let the warm drops ease his throbbing body. But he was troubled by the endless streams of army ants that continued to pour into the camp. He could see them carefully picking their way around the patches of burning grass as they advanced.

By daybreak the men finally succeeded in stemming the tide of army ants. They got rid of the ants still crawling around the camp by shoveling heaps of hot ashes over them. Soon they were all gone.

Later that day, the camp returned to normal. Of the thousands of ants that had overrun the site, many had been killed. Many more had moved on, continuing to devour every living being in their path.

Workers took Dr. Livingstone to the hospital. The doctors treated his terrible ant bites as best they could. After a week or so he was able to return to his work.

WHAT ARE ARMY ANTS?

Army ants are easy to tell apart from ordinary household ants. They are bigger. Their legs are much longer. And they are brown and yellow instead of black or reddish brown.

Army ants are found only in tropical lands. They are of two related types. Those that live in Africa and Asia are called driver ants (or *Anomma*). The kind that live in South and Central America have the name legionary ants (or *Eciton*).

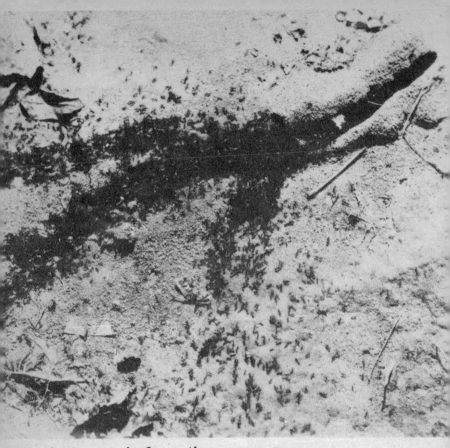

Army ants in formation
Negative No. 222452; photograph by Herbert Lang, courtesy Department
Library Services, American Museum of Natural History

Army ants are so-called because they look so
military when they are on the march. It seems as
if they are following the commands of some general leading his troops into battle. Sometimes they
move in one big mass, as though about to launch
a full-scale frontal attack. Other times they form

long, narrow lines. This formation makes them look like they are trying to flank or surround the enemy.

All ants—including army ants—live in nests and work with other ants. These groups are called colonies. Each colony can contain anywhere from 100,000 up to 30 million ants. The colony is organized so that all the ants share the work that needs to get done.

The colonies of army ants are especially well-organized. Their nests are not permanent, as with most other kinds of ants. And their nests are not dug into the ground or built into mound-like shapes. Instead, army ants make nests out of their own bodies!

The way the nests are made is rather strange. Several ants grab hold of a branch or find a hollow tree trunk. Other ants then attach themselves to the first ones. They lock their long legs together. When they are all in place they form a huge ball. And they cling tightly to each other to make the nest.

Army ants keep this nest for about three weeks. During this time the queen ant is heavy and full of eggs. She stays in a hollow space at the very center of the nest. If the weather is cold, the ants who form the nest pull in closely to protect her. On warm days, they leave plenty of openings for breezes to pass through.

Inside the colony, the queen ant lays up to 100,000 eggs. Within a few days the eggs start to hatch. They change into larvae, which look like tiny white worms or caterpillars.

Each day some army ants leave the colony and march through the jungle hunting for food. Army ants are fussy eaters. They will not eat rotting garbage, the flesh of dead animals, or leaves and plants.

Army ants feed only on living beings that they can kill and eat. Insects—caterpillars, beetles, roaches, and other ants, as well as spiders and scorpions, are what they like best. But they will attack—and eat—any small animal they meet in their march. This includes snakes, lizards, rats, and rabbits!

Each ant that goes out brings back to the nest little bits of any insect or animal it has caught and killed. With thousands or millions of mouths in the colony to feed, there is a constant need for fresh supplies of food.

After about three weeks, most of the eggs the queen laid in this latest nest have gone through the larval and pupa stages. They have become adults. The nest suddenly breaks up. It is time for the entire colony to set out on the biggest raid of all.

In the front ranks are the soldier ants. They are comparatively large creatures, up to 1½ inches long. Their two long, sharp hooked jaws look much like curved swords. By slamming these jaws shut, the ants can chop off the head or legs of almost any insect. They can also open a bloody gash in the skin of any animal or human being.

Behind the soldier ants are hordes of worker ants. These are also called raider ants. Most are less than an inch long. They back up the soldiers in ripping bits of flesh from their prey.

Following close behind are a number of smaller worker ants. They are known as nurse ants because they care for any young still in the larval stage. Slung under their abdomens they carry the small white larvae.

The queen ant brings up the end of the line of march. Much larger than the others, she seems almost too big and heavy to keep up with the troops. Worker ants need to push and pull her along.

After marching through the jungle for about 2½ weeks, the queen starts to swell with eggs again. The colony settles down and forms its nest. And the whole cycle begins once more.

WHAT HAPPENS WHEN ARMY ANTS MARCH?

A march of army ants may be a raiding party on the prowl for food. Or perhaps it's the entire colony heading out to make a new nest. No matter which, smelling, hearing, and seeing this gigantic mass crawling forward is a most terrifying experience!

When army ants are on the go, a very special smell fills the air. Some say it is a sweet, somewhat moldy, odor. Others find it disgusting. They say it is more like the smell of rotting meat.

Then there is the hissing sound of the ants making their way along the jungle floor. It is a soft, mysterious rustling, much like the sound of a gentle rainfall. But those who have heard it say it is the most frightening animal sound they know.

Once army ants start to march, nothing can stop them. They climb up and over bushes and low trees. They go into and through any buildings in their path. They hook their legs together and form living bridges to cross streams. Those that fall into the water come together into little balls. The balls float along until they're thrown up on land and rejoin the march.

Army ants on the march will fearlessly attack any and all living beings—from tiny insects to large animals and humans—who are unlucky enough to be in their path. Their method of attack is unique.

Once army ants are on the victim, they rear up on their back legs and open their jaws wide. Then they drop their bodies and slam their jaws shut. ZAP! The two knife-like blades of the jaws slice deep into the victim's flesh.

The two jaws lock in place. The ants rip and tug at the hide or skin. If the victim is a small insect, just one ant can kill it. For larger insects and animals, many ants climb over the victim. Each one looks for an opening to pull and tear at the flesh.

An attack may last several hours. But from the time the ants start their work, the victim is in mortal danger. When army ants clamp shut their jaws they hold on until either the victim is dead or they are killed. And since there is a thick web of ants in all directions, it is almost impossible to escape.

Army ants are bloodthirsty little creatures, always on the lookout for food. Yet they have not killed as many humans as one might expect. Most humans can outrun these ants. And humans usually can pull off or kill biting ants before they do too much damage.

But there are exceptions. Infants and very young children who are left alone by parents may fall victim to army ant attacks. Individuals who are sick or hunters who are wounded have been killed. Elderly men and women may also be unable to protect themselves. And people who are fast asleep sometimes don't wake up until it is too late.

Humans have studied the habits of army ants. And they have found ways to make use of the ants. Some tribes have used army ants to carry out a sentence of death. Tribesmen have tied prisoners to stakes in the path of army ants and let the ants carry out the execution.

Certain cultures use army ants as a test of bravery. Young couples of South America's Arawak

tribe, for example, must pass the "ordeal of the ants" before they can marry. The tribe elders make three "ant frames." They tightly weave long reeds into 6-inch square mats. Then they capture a number of army ants and place them between the reeds. Only the ants' heads stick out on one side. The close weave of reeds holds them fast.

The elders then press the three frames against the head, hands, and feet of each young person. And the ants do the only thing they can do. They bite! After a short while, the elders remove the ants. The "ordeal" is over. The bride and groom are ready to marry.

Some Africans and South Americans have also put army ants to work as housecleaners. When jungle dwellers learn that army ants are approaching, the villagers move out of their huts and homes. The ants sweep through, killing every rat, roach, and other pest.

The villagers wait patiently until the army has passed through. Then they return to their huts, now spotlessly clean and free of pests.

Would you believe that army ants have also been used to help heal very bad cuts?

Cuts that are too deep and wide to heal themselves are sometimes bound together by army ants. Someone pulls the skin around the wound together and carefully places an army ant on the skin. The ant bites. Its jaws grab on both sides of the cut. The person then snips off the body of the ant. The jaws remain locked firmly in place. They work just like a doctor's stitches! When the cut is healed, the jaws are removed.

Healthy humans can escape army ants. And army ants can sometimes even help humans. Still, it is good to know that army ants are only found in the tropics.

4

WASPS

ATTACK OF THE WASPS

Richard Hall, driver of the Senior Surrey van in Hadley, Massachusetts, was nearly killed on August 23, 1987, by a swarm of angry wasps. Hall was making his last stop after taking several senior citizens on a trip to the shopping mall. At four o'clock he dropped Gertrude Carey at her house at the top of a steep, twisting, five-mile mountain road.

While helping Mrs. Carey in with her bundles, Hall noticed a large wasp nest under the eaves of her porch. Pointing to the nest he said, "I hear they become even more nasty at the end of the summer."

"Oh, they don't bother me," Mrs. Carey answered.

Hall stepped up to the nest to take a closer look. Then he turned away. Suddenly he heard a loud buzzing sound. Scores of angry wasps were streaming out of the nest.

"Hurry, Mrs. Carey!" he shouted. "Get into the house." While she scooted inside, he spun around and ran as fast as he could toward his van.

The wasps buzzed in a fury around Hall as he dashed down the path to the road. Hall flung open the van, hurled himself onto the seat, and slammed the door shut behind him. Luckily, no wasps slipped in at the same time.

Hall knew he had been stung badly. His face, arms, and back hurt a great deal. And he could see the raw sores dotting his skin. Each welt marked a spot where he had been stung. The stings were already beginning to swell and turn red. They felt like burning embers held against his skin.

"I've got to get to a doctor," the young man said to himself. He started the motor and set off in the direction of the nearest hospital. It was several miles away in the city of Amherst.

As Hall raced the van down the zigzag mountain road, a hot, itchy feeling fanned out from the back of his head and moved toward the front of his face. At the same time, his heart began to pound furiously and his tongue got thick and heavy. He also heard a loud whistling in his ears. And he had to gasp for every breath he took.

"I'll never make it," Hall thought as he felt himself growing faint and dizzy. He changed course. Instead of heading to the hospital he steered in the direction of the much closer North Station of the Amherst Fire Department. The station, he knew, had a top-flight rescue team and a well-equipped emergency ambulance.

Minute by minute, Hall grew weaker. At one point, his face went numb. A glance in the rear-view mirror showed that his face was completely swollen and already covered with a rash. His eyes were barely visible above his puffy cheeks.

Hall finally pulled into the fire station. Seeing him struggling to crawl out of the van, two fire fighters rushed to his side. They carried him to the waiting ambulance. Turning on the siren and the flashing lights, they sped off to the hospital.

As they drove, the firemen radioed ahead to the emergency room. When they arrived, two doctors were there to meet the ambulance. Without wasting a second, they gave Hall an injection to fight the effects of the wasp stings.

Within just a few minutes, Hall's cold, numb body began to grow warm and tingling. He started to breathe normally. His heartbeat slowed down.

Eventually Hall recovered. The swelling and rashes cleared up. But as long as he lives, he'll never forget his brush with the killer wasps.

WHAT ARE WASPS?

Wasps are in the same family as bees and ants. Like the others, wasps come in various shapes, colors, and sizes. Most have long, slender bodies and two pairs of wings. The wings are hooked together. They act like a single pair when the insects fly.

Their sleek, shiny bodies are usually steely blue, black, yellow, or reddish. They have three parts—head, thorax, and abdomen. In many kinds of wasps a narrow part, called the "wasp waist," joins the thorax and abdomen.

Wasp

Negative No. 333605; photograph by J.E.T., courtesy Department Library Services, American Museum of Natural History

Most wasps are social. They live in large colonies of between two and three thousand wasps and co-operate with one another. Two of the best-known social wasps—yellow jackets and hornets—are killers.

Other wasps live by themselves. They are called solitary wasps. Solitary wasps do not live in colonies, but build separate nests. Certain kinds make homes in the nests of other insects.

Social wasps live in colonies made up of a queen, female workers, and a number of male wasps. As in all insect colonies, each wasp that lives in the nest has its own work to do. The queen lays eggs. The males mate with the queen and then die. And the workers build the nest, hunt for food, and care for the young larvae.

While some insects live in the same nest for years, most wasp colonies only last for one summer. In the fall the wasps abandon the nest. All the wasps die, except for a number of young queens. The queens find some nook or crack where they can hibernate through the winter.

When the days get longer and the weather warms up in the spring, the queens wake up and crawl out of their hiding places. They get ready to start new colonies.

The queen first builds a new nest. She may tuck it under a porch beam or roof. Or else she may attach it to the limb of a tree or bush, or place it in a hollow tree or even in an old tin can.

To make the nest, the queen bites off bits of old wood and tough plant fibers. She uses her saliva to chew them to a pulp. Then the queen forms the

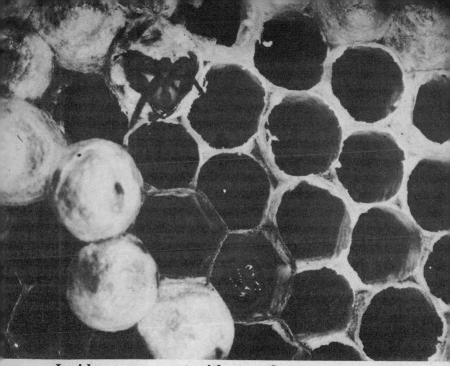

Inside a wasp nest with eggs, larvae, pupae, and adult

Photograph by Runk/Schoenberger, courtesy Grant Heilman Photography, Inc.

mixture into a thin layer that looks and feels like paper. The wasp paper is just like the paper in this book. In fact, it is said that the Chinese first learned how to make paper by watching wasps at work.

Inside the nest the queen makes a number of separate cells. She surrounds each cell with a wall formed of two or three layers of paper.

In each cell the queen lays one egg. When the eggs hatch, they become caterpillar-like larvae that are called grubs. The queen cares for them.

She catches insects, chews them, and feeds them to the larvae.

After two weeks the larvae spin tough cocoons around themselves. They spend the next ten days inside as pupae. When they come out of the cocoon they are full-grown wasps.

Now the queen no longer works on the nest or feeds the larvae. All she does is lay eggs. She lays about once a month—and she lays about 1,500 eggs at one time.

Most of the eggs hatch into female worker wasps. These wasps take over most jobs in the colony. Female workers make the nest bigger by pulling layers of paper away from the inside of the nest wall and adding new layers to the outside. They also find food and feed the larvae.

Solitary wasps behave more like masons than like papermakers. Some make mortar out of mud and saliva. They shape the mixture into little mud nests that look like urns. Some may fasten two or three little nests on one twig. Or they may plaster their nests under porch roofs or in the corners of other structures.

Solitary wasps do not divide the work. Females build the nest and gather the food. When the nest is finished, the wasp flies out to catch caterpillars, spiders, beetles, flies, ants, or other insects for her larvae.

HOW DO WASPS KILL THEIR PREY?

Female worker wasps are the only ones that sting. They use a most deadly stinger. It is a thin, pointed dagger hidden in the rear tip of the abdomen.

When the wasp finds a favorite kind of insect, it jabs its stinger into a certain spot. The spot is located where the venom will paralyze—but not kill—the victim. The prey must remain alive to feed the larvae.

The wasp carries the paralyzed insect back to the nest, which may be some distance away. She places the insect inside a cell where there is an egg. Then she seals it shut and flies off again to catch more insects.

In time, the egg hatches. The tiny larva dines on its paralyzed victim. The larva grows and, in turn, becomes an adult hunter.

Social wasps threaten people more than solitary wasps. There are many more of them. They can be found everywhere throughout the United States. They nest in large colonies. And they tend to be more aggressive.

The female worker wasps will readily attack and squirt venom into anyone who disturbs or annoys them. Wasp stingers do not have barbs. They do not become detached. Therefore, a single wasp can sting a victim several times before flying on to sting someone else.

Social wasps, such as yellow jackets and hornets, are especially dangerous because they live in nests that house thousands. People who disturb their nests invite attacks by swarms of wasps, each one with the ability to sting over and over again.

HOW DO YELLOW JACKETS DIFFER FROM HORNETS?

Experts generally agree that yellow jackets (*Vespula pennsylvanica*) are the boldest of all wasps. And their sting is among the most painful of all insect stings. Once they attack, they keep on stinging until something stops them. And their stings can kill.

Yellow jackets sometimes attack with little reason. Like bees, yellow jackets fly faster than people can run. Swooping and diving just like jet fighters,

these wasps stay on the trail until they land and plunge in their stingers.

And what stings they give! Their stingers are bigger and sharper than those of the bees. That means they can inject more venom with each sting.

Yellow jackets resemble bees. They both have black heads and bright yellow and black stripes on their bodies. Overall, yellow jackets are about two-thirds of an inch long.

The nests of yellow jackets are made of paper, like the nests of all social wasps. Many are in the ground, often in holes dug by small animals. A few are found hanging from trees or in empty boxes or tin cans. Their habit of building nests near humans and being quick to attack make yellow jackets a particularly serious threat to picnickers and others.

Hornets (*Vespula maculata*) have a terrible reputation for attacking humans because they are jittery insects, very intent on protecting their nests. But they are actually slower to swoop down on people and sting than yellow jackets. Their stings, though, can be just as harmful as yellow jacket stings.

Most hornets are a little bigger than yellow jackets. They are dark in color. Their black bodies have white or yellow markings.

Like yellow jackets, hornets make large paper nests from wood and plant fiber that they have chewed. They put their paper nests in trees, shrubs, or buildings. The nests are usually in the familiar round or football shape. They are almost always above ground.

Wasp nest, as seen from the outside
Negative No. 31841; photograph by J. Otis Wheelock, courtesy Department
Library Services, American Museum of Natural History

WHAT CAUSES WASP STINGS?

Wasps mainly use their stingers to capture insects
for food. As for humans, most wasps have an "If
you don't bother me, I won't bother you" attitude.
Humans are not part of the wasp diet.

But wasps are very jumpy and skittish. Someone
bumps into a wasp nest, sits or steps on a nest,
gets too close to a wasp, or traps a wasp in some
clothing—and the wasp gives a painful and dangerous sting.

Anyone stung by a yellow jacket or hornet feels pain right away. The sting swells and turns red. Within about four hours the pain, swelling, and redness start to go down. In a day or so, the sting is nothing more than a bad memory.

Some few people, though, do not get off so lightly. They suffer a bad allergic reaction. It is similar to the allergic reactions that follow bee and ant stings. The symptoms range from mild to severe, depending on how sensitive or allergic the victims are to the chemicals in the sting poison.

Mild cases develop patches of rash or hives. Their skin feels itchy, they have a general sick feeling, and they find themselves more anxious and worried than usual.

People who suffer a moderate reaction may feel any or all of the mild symptoms. In addition, fluid collects under the skin, leading to more general swelling. There is also a tightness in the chest and a wheezing sound with every breath. Other symptoms include pain in the abdomen, nausea, vomiting, and dizziness.

A severe reaction can result in any or all of the mild and moderate symptoms—plus much more. Among them are difficulty in swallowing and speaking and a general weakness. There may also be mental symptoms, such as confusion, fear, anxiety, and great difficulty in concentrating.

In the very worst cases, the victims go into shock. Their blood pressure drops way down, they collapse and lose consciousness. And unless they are given immediate medical care, they can die.

Nationwide, about 50 deaths are blamed on wasp stings every year. But 500 deaths is probably a more accurate number. The symptoms of a bad wasp sting are like the symptoms of a heart attack. Many deaths due to wasp stings get confused with fatal heart attacks.

Wasps are believed to be very intelligent insects. But they are not smart enough to know whether a person means to harm them or not. Therefore, it's a good idea to stay far away from these potential killers.

5

SPIDERS AND SCORPIONS

ATTACK OF THE SPIDERS

One by one, the entire Downing family—Larry and Carol and their two children, Alex, age 12, and Nina, age 9—were bitten by black widow spiders on the same day in August 1989. These freak accidents took place on their family farm some 80 miles outside Stockton, California.

The series of awful events began when Nina went into the barn on that summer morning. She saw a beautiful spiderweb in a corner of the barn. It was glistening with drops of dew in the bright sunlight. Gently, Nina touched the center with her finger.

What Nina didn't see was a shiny black spider, hiding in a corner of the web. It bolted forward, landed on Nina's finger, and nipped her.

The startled child started to scream, more out of fear than pain. The loud cries brought her mother running. Nina pointed to the two tiny red puncture marks on her finger. And she showed her mother the spiderweb.

Wanting to see what kind of spider had bitten Nina, Carol bent over to examine the web. As she poked around, she too suddenly felt the smart of a black widow spider bite.

By now, Larry and Alex had arrived at the barn. Larry grabbed a shovel and banged it down hard on the web. With a single blow he destroyed the web and killed the spider.

Then Larry went on a wild rampage around the barn. He searched out the spiderwebs in all the dark corners. Swinging his shovel, he ripped apart the webs and tried to kill the spiders.

Alex trailed after Larry. He helped his father find webs that were hidden or that he had missed. Then suddenly, within seconds of each other, Larry and Alex cried out. Father and son had touched different black widow webs—and both got bites. Larry's was on his arm, Alex's on his hand.

Although the bites hardly hurt, everyone was frightened. The Downings knew that the bite of the black widow is poisonous. And they had heard that people could die from black widow bites. They decided to drive to a doctor in Stockton, 80 miles away.

Dr. Richard Anton examined the Downings. He moved their legs and pressed their abdomens. "The leg muscles were loose and the abdomen was soft," Dr. Anton reported. "Those were good signs."

Then the doctor asked each one the same questions:

"Has the pain spread out from the bite?

"Do you feel a tightness in the chest?

"Does it hurt when you take a deep breath?"

The negative answers to all his questions made Dr. Anton quite sure that no one was having a bad reaction to the spider bites. But to be sure, he gave each one a shot to counter any effects of the spider poison.

With this clean bill of health from the doctor, the Downings drove back to the farm. Larry said, "It was the happiest ride of our lives!"

WHAT ARE SPIDERS?

Spiders are small animals. They vary in size from tiny—as big as a pinhead, to gigantic—as large as a man's hand.

Many people think spiders are insects. But they're not. They have no wings or antennae. They have only two, not three, body parts. And they don't go through the three stages (larva, pupa, adult) of insects. Spiders are known as arachnids. (See Introduction.)

Almost all spiders spin webs. The webs are made of fine silk thread. Spiders use their webs to catch insects for food.

A spider spins its web with organs called spinnerets. The spinnerets stick out from the rear of the spider's abdomen like tiny fingers. The spider squeezes a liquid out through the spinnerets. As soon as the liquid touches the air it becomes a thin, solid thread.

The spider catches its prey in a curious way. It waits for an insect to get trapped in its web. Then the spider jumps forward. It sinks its two hollow, pointed fangs into the victim. It pumps a poison through the fangs and into the insect's body. The poison either paralyzes or kills the insect.

Spiderweb
Negative No. 336698; photograph by B.J. Kaston, courtesy Department
Library Services, American Museum of Natural History

Mixed in with the poison is a chemical that is similar to the one found in bee venom. The chemical starts to dissolve the insect's body. Spiders don't have teeth or jaws. They can't chew their food. Food must be in liquid form for them to eat. The poison actually digests the insect's flesh. It changes the solid flesh into a liquid.

There are about 30,000 known kinds of spiders. Each one differs slightly in the way it is born, grows, and looks. But all are basically the same.

All spiders are born from eggs. Usually the female lays about 100 eggs at a time. She then spins a sac of silk to enclose the eggs.

The eggs hatch and become spiderlings. No matter when they are born, the spiderlings stay in the egg sac until the weather is warm. Then they force their way out.

Each spiderling first spins a long thread called a drag line. With the drag line it swings free of the egg sac. Then it sets about the business of spinning its own web and catching its first meal.

BLACK WIDOW SPIDERS

Of all spiders, the black widow (*Latrodectus mactans*) is most harmful to humans. Its venom is 15 times more powerful than that of the rattlesnake!

This tiny mischief-maker is only about one half-inch long. It has a small head, a big, round abdomen, and is black and shiny all over. A bright red marking, usually in the shape of an hourglass, can be found on its underside.

Black widow spider with its victim
Negative No. 335466; photograph by J.A.L. Cooke, courtesy Department
Library Services, American Museum of Natural History

Black widows live in every state of the United
States except Hawaii and Alaska. They usually
build their webs down low, near the ground. In-
doors they prefer sheds, garages, barns, and stor-
age buildings where few people enter. Outdoors
they spin their webs under stones, in wood piles,
and beneath loose bark on trees.

Just approach the web of a black widow, and she will probably run away. But touch the web and the spider will bite.

The black widow—like most spiders—is nearly blind. The shaking web makes the spider think that it has trapped an insect. Quite naturally, the spider leaps forward and bites whatever it finds in the web.

Oddly enough, the bite of the black widow hardly hurts at all. It just feels like the prick of a pin or needle. The puncture marks made by the two slender fangs are so small that they are sometimes hard to see. But after an hour or so, the pain gets intense and spreads. And the bite can ache for up to two days.

Victims between 6 and 60 years old who get only one bite are usually in little danger. The black widow only injects a tiny bit of venom when she bites. (Only female black widows bite.) Almost everyone in good health can overcome the effects of the poison.

But the very young and elderly are at great risk. Often the pain moves from the bite to the shoulders, back, and chest. The legs and thighs become stiff and painful to move. Some say it feels like a charley horse over the entire body. Also, the abdomen feels as hard as a board and hurts when touched.

Along with pain and stiffness may come nausea and vomiting, faintness and dizziness, uncontrolled shaking, and paralysis. This may be followed by difficulty in breathing, collapse, and, rarely, death.

About 2,000 people are bitten by black widow spiders every year in the United States. About ten die as a result.

BROWN RECLUSE SPIDERS

The brown recluse (*Loxosceles reclusa*) is another poisonous spider that lives in America. People sometimes call it the violin spider because of the violin-shaped mark on its back.

Found mostly in the south central area of the United States, the brown recluse is a little smaller than the black widow. It ranges in color from tan to dark brown. Most brown recluse spiders make their homes in dry, littered, and abandoned buildings.

Brown recluses are timid little creatures. They try to escape when they sense danger. For that reason, almost all brown recluse bites occur in the same way. The spider crawls into someone's clothes, shoes, or bed. Then, as the person gets dressed, or slides between the sheets, the spider feels trapped. And it bites.

The bite of the brown recluse causes very little pain in the beginning. But gradually matters grow worse. After about two hours the victim feels a very sharp pang. The skin around the bite becomes red and inflamed and starts to blister.

In three or four days the bite turns a deep, dark purple and grows firm and solid. A few days later an open sore appears at the spot. It usually takes about three weeks for the sore to heal and a scar to form.

Meanwhile, the victim runs a fever, has chills, and vomits. The joints ache and feel weak. Red, itchy spots dot the body. In the most serious cases, the venom damages the person's blood cells and kidneys. If there is too much damage, death follows.

ARACHNOPHOBIA
(ah rak nih FOE bee uh)

Little Miss Muffett,
Sat on a tuffet,
Eating her curds and whey.

Along came a spider,
Who sat down beside her,
And scared little Miss Muffett away!

Little Miss Muffett—like nearly everyone else—is scared of spiders. Many tough and brave souls would rather wrestle a cobra or crocodile than let a spider walk across their arm.

But some people have an *especially* strong and intense fear of spiders. They panic every time they see one. They may run away, scream, faint, or behave in other wild and strange ways. Their reactions go far beyond the real danger of being bitten by a spider—which is very slight.

Since so many people suffer from this extraordinary fear of spiders, doctors have given the condition a name. They call it arachnophobia.

People with arachnophobia are deathly afraid of

all spiders. But probably the spider that terrifies them most is the hairy and fierce-looking tarantula (*Lycosa tarentula*).

Tarantulas are among the largest of all spiders. Those that live in the southwestern part of the United States are up to two inches long. But the tarantulas of South America grow to be three and a half inches long! These monsters have a leg spread of up to ten inches!

South American tarantulas eat small animals such as mice, birds, lizards, and frogs. Yet some tarantulas are so gentle that people keep them as pets.

The venom of the tarantula is quite mild. No one has ever died from its bite. But in the past it caused deaths in a very odd way. Individuals who were bitten by the tarantula sometimes danced themselves to death!

During the Middle Ages in Europe, the fear of the tarantula was even worse than it is now. Many believed that the tarantula's venom was very powerful. And they thought that it made people dance about wildly!

Actually, it was the power of suggestion that made those who were bitten by a tarantula whirl about in a dancing frenzy. Madly they spun around and jumped up and down without stop or rest.

After doing this for hours, or even whole days, the dancers collapsed. Some recovered. But others just died of exhaustion. They were not the victims of chemicals in the tarantula's venom. They were really victims of their fear of spiders—of arachnophobia.

SCORPIONS

Scorpions also belong to the class of animals we call arachnids. Yet they don't look anything like spiders. They look more like crabs with two large claws in front.

Unlike crabs, though, scorpions have long, narrow bodies. They are black and yellow in color and measure between one-half and four inches in length.

Scorpion
Photograph by Runk/Schoenberger, courtesy Grant Heilman Photography, Inc.

Perhaps the most frightening part of the scorpion is its long, sharp, curved stinger. It sticks out at the end of a tail-like part of the abdomen. But instead of being in the rear, the tail arches forward, up and over the scorpion's body. And the dagger tip of the stinger points straight ahead.

Scorpions are born from eggs that develop and hatch inside the female's body. The young come out as mini-scorpions. But they are completely helpless. They climb up on the back of the mother and stay there for a few days. After that time they are ready to go off on their own.

Scorpions are night creatures. When it is dark, they hunt for food. During the day they hide from the light under bark, rocks, logs, or piles of dirt.

Scorpions mostly eat large insects, such as beetles, wasps, moths, and crickets, as well as spiders and other scorpions.

First, the scorpion grabs the unlucky bug with its claws. Then it flicks its tail forward faster than the eye can see. And it buries the stinger deep in the victim. Muscles in the tail pump venom out through the hollow stinger.

At the same time, the scorpion crushes and shreds the prey with its two powerful claws. It uses two small fangs on its head to inject a chemical. This chemical is like a digestive juice. It starts to dissolve the captive's flesh. The scorpion can then suck the liquid.

The scorpions' habit of prowling in the dark is dangerous to humans. Scorpions sometimes wander into people's homes at night. Then, when the sun comes up in the morning and it gets light, the scorpions seek a dark place to hide. They often choose a piece of clothing, shoe, bed, closet, or drawer.

What happens when someone puts on the clothing or shoe or uses the bed, closet, or drawer?

The scorpion pounces on the intruder. It flicks forward its deadly stinger. And it pumps poison into the wound.

Different types of scorpions live in warm areas all over the world. In the United States they are found mostly in the hot, dry areas of Arizona and New Mexico. The scientific names of the most dangerous ones from there are *Centruroides sculpturatus* and *Centruroides gertschi.*

Unlike most insects, scorpions live alone. In fact, if you put two scorpions together in a small cage, they will fight. And, sooner or later, one will kill and eat the other!

Scorpion poison is very powerful in its effects on humans. For a long time the Durango scorpion (*Centruroides suffusus*) of Mexico was killing about 2,000 people every year. In recent years, experts have controlled the number of scorpions. And doctors have found new drugs to save the lives of those who are stung. As a result, the number of deaths has been brought way down.

Scorpions will only sting people who touch or bother them. Their venom is very fast-acting. Within minutes, the victim feels sharp, stabbing pains at the site of the sting. Swelling, numbness, and a tingling feeling may follow. Other long-range effects are possible.

Young people suffer much more from scorpion stings than adults. The statistics tell the story:

about one percent of adults die from scorpion stings. Sixty percent of youngsters under the age of five who are stung by scorpions die of their wounds!

Children who are stung become very nervous and restless. Their eye muscles become weak and their eyes shake back and forth. And their blood pressure shoots way up.

Spiders and scorpions are not the only arachnids that are hazardous to humans. Others, including mites and ticks, can make people very sick. But they seldom kill. Among arachnids, only spiders and scorpions are the real killers.

6

FLEAS, FLIES, AND MOSQUITOES

ATTACK OF THE FLEAS

Back in the middle years of the 14th century, people in Florence, Italy, noticed some very strange—and dreadful—happenings. On every street and in every neighborhood of the city men, women, and children were falling sick. One day a person would wake up feeling fine. The next morning the same person would be aching all over and suffering chills and a splitting headache.

Before the day was over, the person would notice a swelling on the neck, in the armpits, or in the groin. At first, the swelling looked like an egg under the skin. But before long it grew to be the size of an orange.

Twenty-four hours later, the swelling had spread. The dull ache had become a terrible tearing and cutting pain. The fever had peaked and the victim was vomiting without stop. Oddly enough, the tongue turned yellow or brown in color.

By the third day, dark blotches had appeared all over the sick person's body. The black spots were an extremely bad sign. Everyone knew that within a matter of hours the victim would be dead.

During the 14th century, millions lost their lives in just this way. They fell victim to one of the most horrid of all diseases—bubonic plague!

The plague is a devastating disease that spreads rapidly and almost always ends in death. The dark spots on the skin gave rise to the common name Black Death.

At first it was thought that the plague came from something in the air. "It must be breathed in," said the doctors of that time. "Why else do so many people fall sick?" They advised folks to hold flowers or spices to their noses to keep out the bad air.

Today we know much more about this deadly disease. It is caused by a killer insect call the Oriental rat flea. This pest can wipe out whole cities. Yet it is only a little bigger than the period at the end of this sentence.

WHAT ARE FLEAS?

Fleas are small, wingless insects. They live on animals and people. And they feed on the blood they suck from these living beings.

Fleas are very flat from side to side. They have small heads and large abdomens in which they store the blood they drink. Their long and amazingly strong back legs let them jump more than a foot in distance and nearly eight inches high. The leaps carry them from animal to man and from animal to animal. Their body shape and powerful legs are ideal for moving quickly and easily through the hairs or fur of any animal.

To get blood, fleas have beaks that work like tiny oil well rigs. With its beak, the flea drills through the skin of the animal. Then it sucks up enough blood to fill its abdomen.

The Oriental rat flea, like other fleas, has no wings and is practically flat. And it has the same remarkable jumping ability.

Originally from Egypt, the rat flea is either brown or black in color. It is named *Xenopsylla cheopis* after Cheops, the builder of the first pyramid.

For food, the rat flea prefers blood from rats. But it will suck blood from any animal, including humans. And that's what makes it such a killer.

Many rats are infected with bacteria known as *Pasteurella pestis*. The bacteria live in the rat's blood. They don't harm the rat. Then along comes a flea. It bites the rat with its long, sharp beak and sucks the rat's blood.

Model of an Oriental rat flea
Negative No. 19411, courtesy Department Library Services, American Museum of Natural History

As the flea sips the blood, it also picks up some bacteria. The bacteria grow and multiply inside the flea's body. Soon there are so many bacteria that they completely choke the flea. The flea cannot swallow anything—not even more blood.

Still, the flea is hungry. It continues to hop about, looking for its next meal. The next target may be a human being. The flea jumps on, digs in its beak, and sips some blood.

But the flea can't swallow the blood because its body is blocked up with bacteria. So it vomits the blood back into the wound. Now, however, some bacteria are mixed in with the blood.

The bacteria start to grow in the human's blood. More and more bacteria clog the bloodstream. The victim begins to notice some swelling. About nine out of every ten people who show these first symptoms are dead within two weeks.

HOW DOES THE PLAGUE SPREAD?

Fleas cause outbreaks of plague by carrying disease-causing bacteria. As they hop around, they move the bacteria from sick rats and humans to healthy ones. In this way, the disease can quickly strike down an entire population. When a disease is so widespread, it is considered an epidemic. An epidemic occurs when many people have the same disease at one time.

The earliest records of a bubonic plague epidemic go back to the year 542 in the ancient mideast. For the following 60 years, the disease spread rapidly from person to person. Over that period it killed about 100 million people!

Large numbers of people continued to die of the plague over the next centuries. But there was no epidemic. Then, in the 14th century, the disease swept across all of Europe. It started in a most bizarre way.

In 1346, an army of Tartars laid siege to a colony of Italian traders in the walled city of Caffa in the Crimea. During the three years of the siege, a plague epidemic infected the Tartar forces. It killed thousands.

Believing that the corpses might carry the disease—and wanting to rid themselves of the dead bodies—the Tartars loaded the corpses on catapults. Then they fired them at the Italians over the city walls. Soon after that, the Italians fought off the Tartars and made their way back to Italy. But with them came some rats that had bitten the infected corpses. These rats now carried some of the deadly plague bacteria.

That did it. Within weeks, the Black Death flared up in Italy. And from there it spread until it raged out of control throughout all of Europe!

About 25 million lost their lives from the plague over the following three years. In Italy and England, which were hit the hardest, about one out of every two people perished. In the rest of Europe about one-quarter of the population was wiped out.

Since then there have been a number of major epidemics of bubonic plague. Some 70,000 people died in the city of London alone between 1664 and 1666. In 1834 there were 30,000 plague deaths in Cairo. Around the globe, about 13 million victims fell in 1891. And over the following years, at least one million people a year succumbed to the plague.

Although there has been no full-scale epidemic in the 20th century, bubonic plague deaths continue even today. Every year a few cases appear in parts of Asia and Africa. There have even been some plague victims in backward areas of the Soviet Union and the United States. Over the centuries, the bubonic plague has claimed more lives than all the wars in history!

The Oriental rat flea can survive under almost any condition anywhere in the world. It is mostly found where many people live in crowded, dirty surroundings. Once these were the slums of big cities. Today it is backward country villages and towns. That's where there are lots of rats. And that's where fleas can hop from victim to victim and spread the disease.

Right now, few people are dying from the plague. Good public sanitation and improved personal hy-

giene have cut the number of infected rats and fleas. Also, doctors now have drugs to treat the diseases.

But the threat of the plague is still with us. For example, a long garbage strike could leave huge piles of trash on the streets. With lots of rotting garbage to feed on, the number of rats would multiply. With more rats, the population of fleas would also increase. A plague could easily get started, but thanks to modern science, the outbreak would probably be stopped before it became an epidemic.

WHAT ARE FLIES?

Flies rank a little below fleas as the most dangerous pests known to humankind. People fear them mainly because they carry germs inside their bodies or on their body hair. Each time a fly bites or touches an object, it leaves some germs behind. The germs can cause serious diseases.

The tsetse fly is one of many types of disease-carrying flies. The name comes from the high-pitched wavering sound of its buzz. Its scientific name is *Glossina*.

Tsetse flies look like common houseflies. The main differences are that the tsetse flies are slightly larger than ordinary flies and are brown and yellow instead of black.

The fly's mouth is shaped like a funnel. The widest part is nearest the head. The thin end, which is used to suck blood, extends downward. In the tsetse fly, the tip of the mouth part is very strong and sharp. It can cut right through a rhinoceros skin or a thick canvas jacket!

Tsetse fly after feeding (note swollen abdomen)
Negative No. 336026; photograph by J.A.L. Cooke, courtesy Department
Library Services, American Museum of Natural History

The tsetse fly sucks blood much like the rat flea.
The fly lands on a human or animal. At the same
time it drops its head. Its sword-like snout pierces
the skin. In a flash it takes a deep sip of blood and
flies off.

All this happens very quickly. By the time the
victim feels anything, the tsetse fly is gone.

As with the rat flea, it's not the bite that kills.
It's what the bite brings. The tsetse fly can be
carrying microscopic organisms called trypanosomes, which in humans cause the disease called
sleeping sickness.

Here's how sleeping sickness spreads: the tsetse
fly bites an animal or person whose blood contains
trypanosomes. The fly sucks the blood. It picks up
the organisms.

The trypanosomes multiply in the fly's body. After about a month, they go into the fly's saliva. From then on the fly infects every person it bites. Each sip of blood injects some organisms into the victim.

The first symptoms of sleeping sickness can come as soon as ten days. Or it can take as long as five years. But sooner or later, the victims start to show signs of the disease.

At first, there is fever, pain, and a very fast heartbeat. Then the symptoms grow much worse. The victims tremble and find it hard to speak. Most can only whisper. After a while, they grow so weak that they can hardly talk or walk at all.

As the days go on, the patients sleep more and more. In time, it becomes almost impossible to wake them. Finally, they go into a very deep sleep, like a coma, and die. The disease kills up to 20,000 people a year.

Sleeping sickness occurs mostly in tropical Africa, usually along lakeshores or riverbanks. For many years, experts have been working to stop or control this disease. They spray chemicals to kill the tsetse fly larvae. They spray other chemicals to sterilize male flies so that they cannot reproduce. And they burn the grass and brush where the flies breed and grow.

So far, they have made some progress. Still, they are always on the lookout for new and better ways to get rid of the fly and the disease it brings. The future of Africa depends, in part, on their success.

WHAT ARE MOSQUITOES?

After fleas, bees, and flies, mosquitoes are the fourth great killer among insects. Mosquitoes spread some of the worst diseases known to man.

Mosquitoes kill the same way as rat fleas and tsetse flies. They pass on deadly germs. When a mosquito bites someone, it leaves the germs behind.

Only female mosquitoes bite. They need sips of animal or human blood for their eggs to develop. These mosquitoes can smell a victim from far away. Then they circle around for a few minutes before settling on the skin. When they land, their touch is so soft that most people don't even feel it.

Mosquitoes usually wait a while before biting. Some think they use this time to find the place where the skin is softest and thinnest.

A mosquito bite is not like a human bite into a hamburger. Mosquitoes cannot open their jaws. They actually stab the victim with a part of their mouth. The mouth part contains six hollow needles.

Through one of the needles, the mosquito drips saliva into the wound. The saliva does not let the blood clot. It keeps it liquid while the mosquito is drinking. Through the other needles it sucks up the blood.

Very often the saliva contains more than chemicals to stop clotting. It may also hold disease-causing germs. As the mosquito flies around, it bites some people who are sick. There are germs in their blood. The mosquito picks up some of these germs. The germs grow inside the mosquito. Then,

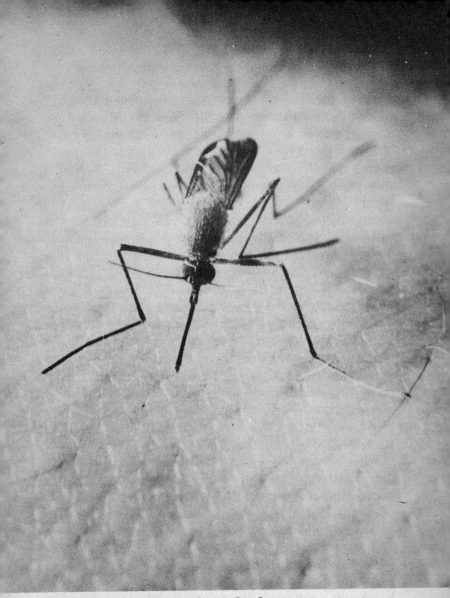

Female mosquito ready to feed
Photograph by Runk/Schoenberger, courtesy Grant Heilman Photography, Inc.

when the mosquito bites other people, it passes on the germs.

The germs grow quickly in the bloodstream of the new victim. Before long, the person may be sick with one of ten serious diseases that mosquitoes can carry.

Today, one-half of the entire world population is sick with malaria—a disease carried by the *Anopheles* mosquito. Around one million will die of malaria this year alone!

The *Anopheles* mosquito mostly lives in the hot, humid areas of Africa, Asia, South and Central America, and southern Europe. It is pretty well gone from the United States.

The *Anopheles* mosquito spreads a tiny organism known as *Plasmodium*. This is the organism that causes malaria. The *Plasmodium* enters the person's red blood cells—and bursts them open. The person falls sick with malaria. The symptoms range from a hot, raging fever, to chills and violent shaking. In some cases the trembling can be so strong that the patient's bed actually rattles and moves across the floor! After a while, the fever and chills stop. Later they come back again. This goes on—starting and stopping—until the malaria finally claims the person's life.

The only way to get rid of malaria is to wipe out the *Anopheles* mosquito. The best way to do this is by destroying the swamps where they breed. While some progress has been made, malaria still remains a major killer.

People have been more successful in battling the *Aedes aegypti* mosquito. This mosquito is the one

that carries the yellow fever virus. Until recently, yellow fever was responsible for millions of deaths.

Aedes aegypti mosquitoes lay their eggs in open containers of water—barrels, buckets, and cans. By sealing or emptying these water holders, government officials were able to cut down the number of breeding places. With fewer places to breed, the number of mosquitoes and deaths from the disease has fallen.

The *Aedes aegypti* mosquito picks up the yellow fever virus from an infected person or monkey. After a few days, it can transmit the disease. The virus-laden mosquito continues to infect people with the virus as long as it lives.

Symptoms of yellow fever start about five days after the mosquito bites someone. Along with the high temperature comes restlessness and severe bone aches throughout the body. A few days later, the temperature suddenly drops and the skin turns yellow. But the break in temperature doesn't last long. Another three days or so and the person is sicker than ever. Death usually follows.

In 1985, a ship arrived in Houston, Texas, carrying a load of tires from Asia. Somewhere, hidden on the ship or in the cargo, were some Asian tiger mosquitoes (*Aedes albopictus*). They got this name because of their orange stripes.

Since then, these mosquitoes have spread to more than 17 states in the eastern half of the nation. And they have brought with them a number of killer diseases. One is dengue fever, which causes a rash and severe pains in the bones, joints and muscles. Another is encephalitis, an inflammation of the brain that mainly strikes children and is sometimes fatal.

Most people know and fear killer bees, fire ants, yellow jackets, and black widow spiders. But truth is stranger than fiction. Fleas, flies, and mosquitoes may be more lowly. But they are even more deadly killers!

Comic books, horror stories and science fiction tell about deadly killers of all sorts. Yet, killer bugs are far more frightening than anything that writers can imagine. Killer bugs are scarier than make-believe killers for one reason—they are REAL!